New Zealand Odyssey

NEW ZEALAND ODYSSEY

A graphic journey by Don Donovan, illustrator,
and Euan Sarginson, photographer

HEINEMANN REED

To Pat and Min; Philippa, Alice, Susannah and
Finlay; and in memory of Ruby and Sheila.

Our very special thanks to David Heap, who
made us do it.

Published by Heinemann Reed,
a division of Octopus Publishing Group (NZ) Ltd,
39 Rawene Road, Birkenhead, Auckland. Associated
companies, branches and representatives throughout
the world.

© 1989 Don Donovan and Euan Sarginson

First published 1989
Designed by Euan Sarginson
Production by Pages Literary Pursuits
Typeset by Rennies Illustrations Ltd
Printed in Singapore

CONTENTS

The Reason Why

I grew up in South London during the Second World War, a part of my life punctuated by two spells in the Surrey countryside as an evacuee. Both occasions coincided with quiet periods of the civilian war. I was in London when the bombing was at its worst and in the country on Hitler's days off! But my interludes as a rustic were of great value, for they planted in me a seed of love of the less crowded places, a seed that finally flowered when I came to New Zealand in 1960.

Twenty-nine years later the spell of New Zealand, under which I fell as we steamed into Port Nicholson with the dawn sun hitting the toy-town houses of Seatoun, still works on me; never for one day have I regretted coming to the land of which I am now a committed citizen.

Fate inevitably led me into the company of Euan Sarginson, with whom I have both worked and had a deep friendship since the earliest of my days in Christchurch. Our friendship and my profound respect for his talents have grown, even though we have not lived in the same city for many years.

Our views of New Zealand are compatible: mine still sharpened by the objectivity of a new chum, his thrown into relief by useful periods out of the country that have allowed him to observe old favourites through the eyes of a returning expatriate.

What we have attempted to do in this book is to share with you our delight in the ordinary things of New Zealand that are seen but not examined by us average New Zealanders every day of the week. For this is a book for New Zealanders. It is not aimed at tourists unless they are interested in mementoes more challenging than the usual pretty, scenic takeaway.

Through Euan's camera and my pen and brush we have compiled a selfish, idiosyncratic collection of images, most of which have taken our fancy during random wanderings between Cape Reinga and Bluff since early 1986.

Some of the images are more appropriate to the camera than the brush; others the opposite. The illustrator has the option of including or omitting detail, enlarging it, moving it, or emphasising it. He, like a caricaturist, is able to point out the essence of the object, to focus on its personality and character. There is much trickery, and I shall be found unrepentant if keen viewers discover differences in detail between the illustration and its subject.

It might be thought that there can be no trickery in the camera. While it is true that Euan cannot leave out an unwelcome telegraph pole, his capacity for seeing something in the landscape that others cannot see is highly developed. His means of trickery lie in manipulation of shape through a range of lenses, light through cunning use of filters, and texture through the scientific shenanigans of the processing laboratory. What you see is what was there — but maybe you didn't see it the same way as we did!

When we set out on our New Zealand odyssey we sought features of town and country, building and landscape that would beckon to us and insist on inclusion as representatives of the real New Zealand. Like music-lovers who protest they know nothing about music but know what they like, we set out with the idea that we didn't know what we'd draw or photograph but we'd know it when we saw it!

We liked a lot. We drew and photographed about

6

five times more subject matter than appears in this book. We're only too aware of how much we left behind, and if you cannot find your favourite town hall, war memorial or decaying boatshed we apologise.

Our country's buildings are not old enough to be 'of the land'. In the main they are on it rather than of it. Regrettably the pre-European colonisers built with materials that could not last. Therefore, with the exception of much-eroded earthworks, the oldest structures are European. Even these, unless in advanced states of decay, sit on the landscape as very obvious artefacts, although many of the old wooden structures have learned to bend to the forces of nature. There is great delight to the eye in once-parallel pit-sawn planks now undulating like exposed subterranean strata.

There is also great delight in structures whose charm comes from practicality rather than artistry. Early pioneers needed roofs over their heads. In providing themselves with protection they often produced elegantly simple huts and houses that still survive today; their verticals are not, their paint peels or is non-existent, their roofs rust in glorious ochres, and they cry out to the water-colour box.

Conversely we have developed warm affection for those earnest community fathers who found it necessary to reassure themselves that God was in his heaven and all right with the world by commissioning the most pompous banks, town halls, municipal chambers and monuments imaginable! On close examination it is amazing how many provincial pufferies are fronts in dressed stone (or, better, timber made to look like stone) and backs in rusting corrugated iron or peeling weatherboard. In early New Zealand there was clearly just as much difficulty in balancing idealism with finances as there is today, though one suspects that Westport's municipal chambers will outlast the mirrors overlooking Auckland's Grafton Gully.

New Zealand Odyssey has been divided into nine sections of some, to my mind, geographical logic. Although there are illustrations from all over the country, there was no attempt to be fair and even-handed in their apportionment. Some areas, some towns, some land shapes are rich in their appeal; others are lean.

There was no intention to represent either young or old. There is more old than young because old has offered more interest. The land, of course, is ageless.

No attempt has been made to update things that have changed since they were photographed or drawn. Although almost all of the pictures were completed after April 1986, some of their subjects have already disappeared or altered. Fast-changing cities like Auckland or Wellington see mushrooms grow and die overnight, whereas those towns whose populations are diminished or whose fortunes are failing tend to present airs of timelessness, since their buildings are neither demolished nor replaced.

Taste is in the mind of the individual. It is arrogant, we feel, to dictate the boundaries of good or bad taste. In conventional terms, New Zealand's artefacts exhibit more bad taste than good. Public sign-writing, for example, is generally appalling. To inflict a whole building painted by and for a multinational fizzy drink manufacturer on the inhabitants of Reefton is an affront. To present to the visitors and citizens of Rotorua a whole street of motels each more grotty than its neighbour is, to say the least, inconsiderate. But we have set taste aside. We have simply looked at things and chosen or rejected them depending on whether or not they took our fancy.

This book is, in effect, an expression of endearment and a token of thanks to our homeland. New Zealand is incomparable. And it has, so far, overcome all attempts to destroy it. Despite the evidence of human activity everywhere (and that is mainly what this book is all about) one gets the distinct impression that the land is winning. The buildings and other structures are all so temporary. Wind, weather, salt, flood, earthquake, wood-louse, borer, frost and fire would lose little time putting these islands back where they were 1 600 years ago if humankind were to leave.

And when all is said and done there is no greater vandal than nature. Imagine what the conservationists would have had to say if people, rather than nature, had destroyed the Pink and White Terraces!

We love this land. This book says so.

Don Donovan
Auckland 1989

7

Omanaia Methodist Church, 1884.

8

North of the Bombay Hills

NORTHLAND, AUCKLAND

Northland has a warm, damp, wistful smile, occasional gaiety flickering around its edges where, especially to the east, the people of Auckland play summer games along the ribbon of beaches facing the Pacific Ocean.

Ghosts are everywhere. They rise up in the humid mists of primeval rain forests, they hiccup in every small town's Masonic Hall; they stalk, affronted, through neglected farms littered with rusting American car wrecks.

The long, slim body of the northernmost peninsula lies like a Siamese cat on its back, indolently exposing its belly to the sun. The farther one travels up it the more tantalising are the sea views that either sparkle like a shattered windscreen or lie, sultry, under scudding cloud, gleaming like beaten pewter.

There, at the top, is the lighthouse everyone comes to see. Just an ordinary lighthouse, but with a unique place in geography, for a straight line north touches nothing but the odd island before it reaches the Arctic.

Euan and I travelled separately to Northland. He took his family in the Volkswagen Camper they wear like an old overcoat. Having paid due homage to the Cape Reinga lighthouse, he chatted up a tourist-coach driver and arranged to follow him carefully south along the tricky sands of Ninety Mile Beach.

They set off: a coach, the Sarginsons and another coach. Euan diligently followed his leader and it wasn't until they'd done a few figure eights and odd circles, and realised that the passengers in both coaches were having the time of their lives that he caught on

to the fact that the jokers in the VW were the floor show for the day . . .

Parts of the north have the look of old cultivation. Missionary energy and zeal left fields, hedges and stone walls reminiscent of Wiltshire downland. Evangelical purity and colonial dignity produced the simplest yet most elegant of buildings — Waimate North, Kemp House and the Waitangi Treaty House.

Tourism puts unwarranted pressures on the Bay of Islands. Were it not for the seafront houses and a narrow carriageway between them and the sea, Russell would have lost its charm years ago.

Fortunately there is a surviving proportion to the Russell seafront that makes it unique. Along its few hundred metres architectural history is well preserved, with Pompallier House as its climax.

Whangarei is a late developer and has yet to show any real character, but nature comes to its rescue with Mt Manaia and friends to divert the eye from dullness.

Kaitaia is the epitome of parochialism. The brash pride of this provincial town is embodied in a welcome sign at the north end that's so bad it's good! Every service organisation imaginable displays its welcoming badge just a step from one of the most comprehensive gnomes' gardens I've ever seen.

In distinct contrast the Hokianga towns of Kohukohu and Rawene, though a little depressed, maintain the dignity and graciousness of old age. These are the termini of the Hokianga Harbour Vehicular Ferry which plies in no great haste these ancient, mystical waters. While saying reluctant farewells to their youth, they are fossickers' towns, full of old gems, quietly accepting the onslaught of nature; yet fascinating. It is easy to run out of time here. Night seems impatient . . .

Northland has suffered greatly during its long history of human habitation. Vast areas were clear-felled then put into pasture only to go back into scrub as farming entered a cyclical depression. The scrub areas are lonely; undecided whether to start the great journey back into bush or await a rural renaissance. Yet in this heavily modified landscape, there remains the large, untouched kauri forest, a dynasty of giant survivors who have come into their inheritance — conservation.

Travel through the forest becomes dull and wearisome after the first impressive miles, and it is a relief to break out into the southern farmland, the faded stone of Dargaville and the salt marshes of the vast Kaipara Inlet, glinting old gold in the sunset.

South of Helensville in the west, or Warkworth to the east, the pace begins to quicken. Traffic thickens. On low cloud nights the glow of Auckland reflects wanly beyond the Riverhead State Forest or the Albany hills.

The sea dominates Auckland, wasp waisted between the Waitemata and Manukau Harbours (the latter fighting a desperate battle against pollution). One of the world's most sprawling cities, to the rest of New Zealand it seems as brash and gauche as a large, uncontrollable dog.

Auckland grows, and it grows. Architectural nightmares are reflected in mirror blocks alongside the classics, some of which, mercifully, still survive. The mirror blocks may themselves be nightmares but by no means all of them; they flash, gold, *eau-de-Nil*, silver, green, pink — and because the hand of the glazier shakes as readily as Omar Khayyam's potter's, the city blocks distort delightfully all they reflect.

In recent years the protection of old buildings has become fashionable — almost to a fault. It is, perhaps, better to over-protect, but many of the outcries over demolition of the old but not necessarily good have bordered on the hysterical. Enough of the good stuff will survive. Enough, certainly, to fill another book with architectural jewels we've missed, left out, or not yet considered.

Nature cannot be overshadowed by man — even in Auckland. Volcanic cones, much modified in shape by Maori terraces and spiral grazing, are prominent in all directions, the sea is always in the background and somehow or other, the low, green pie-crust of dormant Rangitoto seems to dominate the city like a punishment waiting to be administered.

Despite its sprawl, Auckland is never far away from the country, as the long, lean belt of the Southern Motorway proves. A dangerous highway, it seems to affect its users with the same mysterious compulsion that sends lemmings over cliff edges. It is a road best left behind as it curls and undulates through factory lands, suburban housing estates and eventually the wondrous greens and umbers of south Auckland.

To the west, across rolling town-milk-supply country, past the rumbling steel mills, lies an unfriendly cliff-walled coast. To the east is the western side of the Tamaki Strait and Firth of Thames where, suddenly, Auckland seems a million miles away and the waders, on their red, knitting-needle legs, stride through the reedy cockle beds and wail to a horizon indistinct in a summer haze.

Cape Reinga.

Cape Reinga lighthouse.

On Ninety Mile Beach.

North end,
Ninety Mile Beach.

Kaeo Post Office.

Corner of a Maori cemetery, Mangamuka.

Oruaiti, Northland.

14

Old Masonic Hall, Kohukohu.

Awanui.

Rawene Court House.

By the ferry ramp, Rawene.

Rawene.

Herekino.

Pareokawa.

The Moorings, Russell.

Russell waterfront.

Wooden headboard at St John the Baptist, Waimate North.

Treaty House, Waitangi.

Wainui.

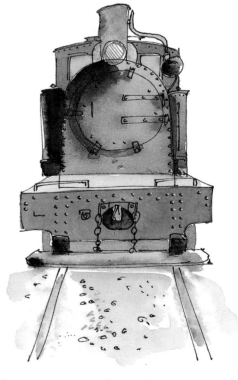

The power unit of Opua's tourist train.

Kemp House, Kerikeri, 1822.

West of Matauri Bay.

Whatoro.

Waipu.

Could be anywhere, but this highway vendor is just south of Whangarei.

Whangarei Town Hall.

The Grand Establishment, Whangarei.

Hikurangi.

At Whakapara. Racial tension or just plain vandalism?

Matakohe.

The archetypal country fire station.

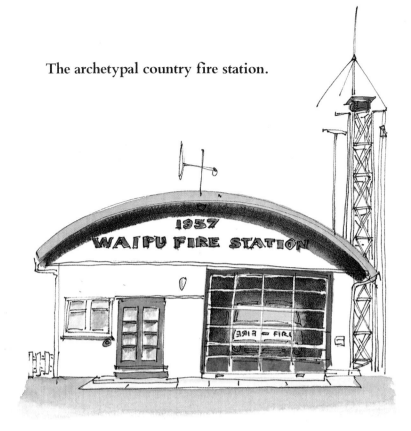

Oakleigh.

Paparoa.

Confusion at Kamo.

More confusion — Kaipara district.

31

Wayby, near Wellsford.

Portland cement works.

Private beach at Pakiri.

Creative spelling near Brighams Creek.

FRUIT & VEGES ...SALE...

TOMATOES BOX $3

TOMATOES $1.50 KG

OPEN

TOMATOES
POTATOES
CAPSICUM
LETTUCE
CUCUMBERS
CABBAGE
GRAPES
BEANS
BROCCOLI
KUMARA
CAULIFLR
SILVERBEET

BROCCOLI
CLOSEING SALE

DANGER
flammable Gas
KEEP CLEAR

Rustic LPG shed, Helensville.

Helensville.

Helensville Quality Meats

LIBRARY
EST. 1865

Kaukapakapa.

Broomfield House, Warkworth, 1870.

Warkworth Masonic Hall.

36

Catsablanca
BOARDING CATTERY
Prop. Phone 413-9392

For a tabby Bogart? Greenhithe.

Dargaville Post Office.

Near Muriwai . . .

. . . coaches called 'home'.

SUPPORT THE TOUR

SUBVERT THE TOUR

Differences of opinion . . .

. . . near Warkworth.

At the time this was drawn, these Edwardian shops in Queen Street were quietly falling apart while their fates were being debated. In 1989 they began a new life as 'Chinatown'.

Professional graffiti, Bowen Street, Auckand.
Originally a synagogue, then an operatic society
hall, it became a bank in 1989.

One glimmer of wit on an illiterate wall, Parnell.

Auckland.

Randolf Street.

Gentlemen's convenience and bus shelter, Symonds Street.

Jervois Road, Ponsonby.

'K' Road.

11 Karaka Street, Newton.

Chelsea Refinery wharf.

Former Grey Lynn Borough Council offices, Ponsonby, 1889.

Princes Street, Auckland.

THE FRANK SARGESON CENTRE
THE GEORGE FRASER GALLERY

**Austral-Mediterranean town houses,
Napier Street, Freemans Bay.**

45

46 Parnell Road (younger than it looks!).

Mt Eden Road, Auckland.

50 Ponsonby Road.

Union Street, Auckland.

Mission Bay *olé*.

The old Auckland Club, Shortland Street.

508 Queen Street.

39 Elliott Street.

Scotland Street, Freemans Bay.

49

Green and Gold

COROMANDEL, BAY OF PLENTY, ROTORUA, TAUPO, WAIKATO

This enormous land tract might be titled 'South of the Bombay Hills' were it not for the fact that it has its own southern boundary. A quite arbitrary one. In the mind of the author. For his convenience . . .

'Green and Gold' because, despite the azures of the Bay of Plenty, the whole region is typified by those two earth colours. Ochre would be more appropriate than gold but I have in mind the auriferous Coromandel Peninsula as much as the yellow-brown loams of the Waikato.

As with most places rich in minerals, the Coromandel hints of arcane treasures as yet undiscovered. It bears the scars of honest exploitation and, worse, scars of tourist-driven deceit.

Attempts to dolly up Coromandel township for the tourists have adulterated the old charm of the place. This has not happened in Thames simply because the tourist has not yet loomed large in the minds of Thames's city fathers.

Everywhere the conservation movement is in evidence, fighting hard to stop mining. A sad irony is that while they revere the old Martha mine pumphouse — an antique symbol of their present-day target — they appear to have overlooked urban despoliation caused by clumsy cosmetic surgery.

I visited Coromandel twice. The first time, with Euan Sarginson, we were so disappointed that we came away with nothing to record. A second look, a different approach, yielded satisfactory evidence of past dignity.

We were conscious that away on the east side, Pauanui discreetly shuffled its kaleidoscopic colours, Remuera-by-the-sea . . .

The Bay of Plenty, washed by the Pacific's kinder waves, faces the sun with a middle-class smile. The rewards of its agricultural gifts seem to have sanitised it, made it mediocre, *nouveau riche*. There was little to stop us between Waihi and Opotiki except for the gracefully decaying Katikati railway station and the cluster of buildings that includes and surrounds 'The Elms', one of New Zealand's oldest homes. It was originally a house of the Church Missionary Society. It now provides a good reason to visit Tauranga.

And Opotiki provides a good reason to visit the Bay of Plenty, for just as you reach its eastern boundary and feel a surfeit of sweetness, Opotiki reminds you that there's an older, tougher, more genuine New Zealand lurking on the fringe.

Perhaps the recently gained — and, by many, more recently lost — prosperity farther west has never reached Opotiki. Perhaps there was no haste to knock down the old and throw up the new. Because here there are characterful buildings on every street, every corner.

Under all there is a sinister side. Something to do with man's inhumanity to man, a severed head, gouged eyes, the blood of a missionary drunk from a desecrated chalice and, later, retribution.

I contemplated the Church of St Stephen the Martyr, shuddered, and headed off in a different direction.

Rotorua and all its thermal ambience is part of a terrestrial alimentary tract that rumbles, gurgles, bubbles and occasionally explodes anywhere between Mt Ruapehu and White Island.

The whole district has been a mecca for tourists — probably since the first Polynesian caught a whiff of its supposedly health-giving sulphurous miasma. Of all its glories, to my mind, the Elizabethan look-alike, built by the government as a bath house in 1906 and styled 'Tudor Towers', stands out. It is magnificent. Why, in heaven's name, did they go Tudor, halfway around the world and over 300 years after the event? Whatever the motivation, they did it very well; unlike 'motel gothic' — but more of that later.

If Thomas Hardy had written about New Zealand his 'Vale of the Great Dairies' would have been the Waikato. My best-ever view of it was from the top of the Kaimai Range, returning north from Tauranga on State Highway 29. This particular day in spring the air felt therapeutic. I stood high, caressed by the mildest of breezes, feeling quite spiritual and extraordinarily grateful for the gift of life. On the farthest horizon, smudged by violet distance, lay Mt Pirongia; to the south, Otorohanga, Te Kuiti and the Rangitoto Range; and away to the right, north, the flatlands and straight roads that border the hinterland of the Thames Firth, with Hamilton — distinguished only by the Waikato River — and the threat of Auckland beyond. Stunning.

In detail, later, I found much to love in the honest hamlets and townships of the Waikato. These settlements were born of necessity — to serve their farming communities. They are proud yet unassuming; simple, straightforward, no-nonsense. Matamata, Waharoa, Morrinsville, Maramarua . . . their names murmur like the bees that harvest their clover pollen. They have a pace as measured as the pulsations of the

Tudor Towers, Rotorua.

51

milking machine or the deliberate forward steps of a browsing Friesian.

The towns that dot State Highway 1 and the Main Trunk railway line, north of Hamilton, share, with farming, other *raisons d'être*. Huntly, a tight little town, famous for bricks and coal and now its flashy new power station; Meremere, in the water meadows, home to an older power station, which, unashamedly and fascinatingly, exposes its engineering for all the world to see. Ngaruawahia, junction of the Waikato and Waipa Rivers, heavy with the presence of ancient Maori; important, serious.

I confess a special relationship with the southern Waikato where it merges with the King Country, for it is there that I find the nearest shingle trout streams to Auckland. There are the ultimate dairy towns — Te Awamutu, Kihikihi, Otorohanga — where the surrounding paddocks are lush, firm and marbled by a thousand waterways.

Oddly enough for the illustrator of a book mainly concerned with structures, my favourite Waikato town is Cambridge — and the reason is its trees. They make the town feel friendly and mature. They say something good about the inhabitants. They help the buildings of Cambridge put their best feet forward.

There's no doubt that even though the late 1980s might have brought some hardship to the rural community, Cambridge has been, and may still be, a source of great wealth. One look at the horses is all you need!

Somewhere to the south-east of Cambridge there's a race of people whose skin is bark and in whose veins runs sap. They live in the timber towns, Tokoroa and Putaruru, and the Kinleith Mill is the altar upon which they offer their existence. Here in the heart of rural New Zealand an industrial complex of over 230 hectares pours smoke and steam into the thin, blue air, scribbling across the sky in all the shades of grey from black to white. It's impressive. More so because it's surrounded by pasture. It's also a reminder that the wealth of our country comes, more often than not, from the land, not the city.

Far in the west, Raglan, a bustling little seaside town whose main street is elevated in status by being a dual carriageway beset by exotic palms, has the silliest name imaginable. It's named after Lord Raglan of Crimea fame, under whose command the Light Brigade performed an act almost as dangerous as driving on Auckland's Southern Motorway.

Shingle plant near Mercer.

52

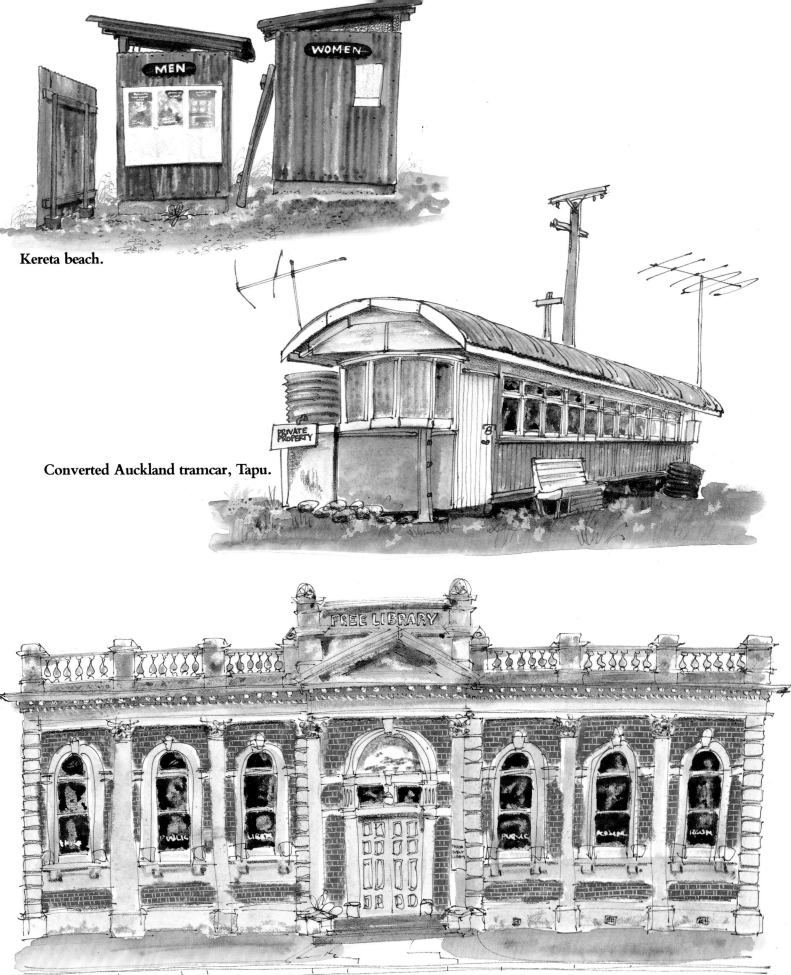

Kereta beach.

Converted Auckland tramcar, Tapu.

Thames Public Library, lovingly restored with brick veneer.

53

Thames-Coromandel District Council, Coromandel area office — the best thing left.

Thames School of Mines Mineralogical Museum — elegant as a baked potato.

**Thames: Priceless
corrugated.**

**Thames woodstone.
Disappeared 1987.**

Coromandel wharf.

Scrubcutter's whare, Waiaro.

All Saints' Anglican (Maori), Manaia.

Kuaotunu.

56

Inspired post office architecture, Whitianga.

Elderly, dignified pumps
at Colville.

Colville.

Coromandel.

Katikati derelict railway station.

Waikino.

Martha Mine pumphouse, Waihi.

Karangahake.

Paeroa Maritime Park.

Motuhora
Island.

Kihikihi Town Hall.

Cambridge.

Huntly power station.

60

West of Pirongia Mountain.

National Hotel bottle store, Cambridge.

Kinleith.

63

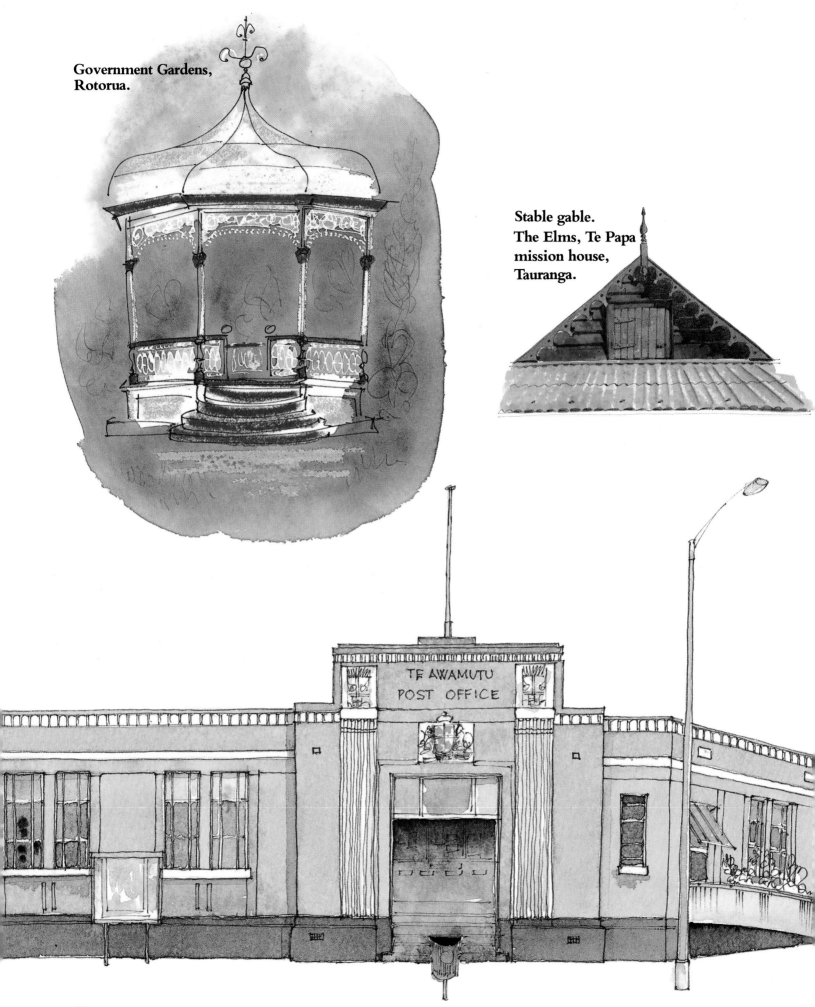

Government Gardens,
Rotorua.

Stable gable.
The Elms, Te Papa
mission house,
Tauranga.

TE AWAMUTU
POST OFFICE

64

Motel Gothic. Fenton Street, Rotorua.

Sunrise Country

EAST CAPE, UREWERA, POVERTY BAY

In company with a few small islands, New Zealand's East Cape shares the distinction of being first in the world to see the sun each day. The sun may not realise this artificial fact — unless its rays feel a slight bump as they cross the international date-line.

I visited East Cape nervously. Our newspapers at the time of my trip were full of fearful stories about terrorism in Ruatoria. A wave of racial awareness was sweeping the country. Maori were insisting on rights embodied in the Treaty of Waitangi. I had a new, sleek, sporty motor car . . . Like a Mr Toad, I had looked forward to motoring through the East Cape area but wondered whether I'd ever be seen alive again!

What piffle! At all the places I visited, every town, village, meeting place, I saw more smiles and waves of greeting than anywhere else in New Zealand.

It was July 1987, before the devastation of a later cyclone. I was driving somewhere near Cape Runaway when I was confronted with a sea of cattle wider than the road and stretching away as far as I could see. In the vanguard rode an elderly Maori wearing a khaki Swanndri, a knitted hat and sucking on a misshapen, hand-rolled cigarette. He led a second horse, and around their legs a pack of dogs weaved and waggled as only New Zealand sheep dogs can. There was a pig, too, and the cattle came in all shapes, sizes, genders and ages.

'That's a flash car,' he said, by way of greeting, peering into the open sunroof from the lofty perch of his docile mount.

'A reward for a lifetime of hard work,' my brave reply.

'That'll be all right then,' by way of forgiveness.

I elicited from him the information that the herd was on its way to Mercer, where they expected to arrive in November. He had a bet on with a drover bringing another mob behind as to who would arrive in Mercer with the most fattened beast!

Freedom of expression. Potts Avenue, Opotiki.

Later, having driven through a river of cattle manure, I confronted the second mob and a taller, leaner, more weather-beaten cattleman. He told me they'd come from Gisborne.

The third and final polymorphous mass of steaks-on-the-hoof was tailed by a younger version of the two earlier drovers. He, too, led a second horse, was surrounded by dogs and had a pig. He told me they had left Gisborne in March of that year! Gisborne to Mercer by way of East Cape; a journey from March to November; a journey where haste would be counter-productive, for these drovers intended that their charges should arrive at Mercer heavier than when they left Gisborne, fattened by the roadside grazing.

'What are the pigs for?' I called as I drove away. He smiled and waved but I missed what he said. I guess they enjoy bacon for breakfast now and then.

It was this experience, two days from Auckland, that put my nervousness to rest. This, I realized, was a different country. Time was measured differently and even though the brooding Raukumara Range and the mist-hung Urewera forests beyond might seem hostile, the coast road had a warmth for every traveller.

The Volkswagen-Camper-clad Sarginson family made the same trip later, after Cyclone Bola had devastated the whole region, turning every little stream into a foaming brown torrent. They found a no less friendly welcome and their enthusiasm for East Cape was boundless, but they were sobered by the scars of natural fury, slipped hillsides, fallen trees, washed-out bridges and piled-up debris, held by distorted fences.

That part of East Cape that borders the eastern Bay of Plenty is dominated by high, bush-covered hills, here and there cloven by misty gorges hinting of a hard life beyond. It is a narrow littoral road punctuated by church-centred settlements, maraes, and those *bijou* beaches where streams run into the sea. Once past Te Araroa — the friendliest of all welcomes — and East Cape itself, there is more breadth and the landscape softens.

It is here that one feels most keenly New Zealand's remoteness from the rest of the world. To the right the crumpled hills; to the left, Chile, thousands of leagues beyond the empty horizon. I saw no ships; yet there must have been ships in abundance in times past, for the size of the derelict freezing works in Hicks Bay and the businesslike cluster of wharfside buildings in Gisborne suggest much mercantile marine movement.

And one of the most thrilling finds for one who loves detailing brickwork in water-colour was the

now unused New Zealand Shipping Company building at the northern end of Tokomaru Bay.

It's ironic that the first part of Aotearoa sighted by British seamen should have been Poverty Bay, for the Gisborne and East Cape areas have the lowest proportion of Pakeha. The Maori population is between one-third and one-half, diluted in summer by an influx of holidaymakers breathing the clean air of the Pacific coast and centring on Tolaga Bay, whose prominent inn is about as fitting in these surroundings as an apple strudel at a hangi.

Poverty Bay is an appellation to which Gisborne gives the lie. While the city seems to be the dramatic focus of droughts and storms it does, nevertheless, give off an air of faded comfort. It is a middle-aged town, middle class and very provincial. It clings to the honour of Captain Cook's 'discovery' by boldly marking its main street with basket-like models of three-masted barks — perhaps their best *Endeavours* — mounted on poles at the bases of which appear to be

Candlewick hills, Hawai.

old tyres from heavy earth-moving machinery. These are painted yellow, filled with soil and planted with shrubs. Waste not want not . . .

I was conscious, while winding north-west from Gisborne into the hills, that I was going to ignore one of the most mysterious and least explored parts of New Zealand. Those comparatively few travellers who cross Urewera country see only Lake Waikaremoana and the forests bordering Route 38, but perhaps may dream, as I do, of Te Kooti's skirmishes with colonial forces in the tortuous valleys beyond. Our search for structures and the hand of man on the landscape tends to lead us away from such romance. Tracks criss-cross the map of Urewera — but no roads. Here, I'm sure, are meeting houses, huts, and rickety bridges that might tempt the artist's hand or the photographer's hovering finger; but we did not seek them.

Truth to tell, the Urewera feels like hallowed ground.

Prohibition, Raukokore.

Opotiki halls.
Masonic . . .

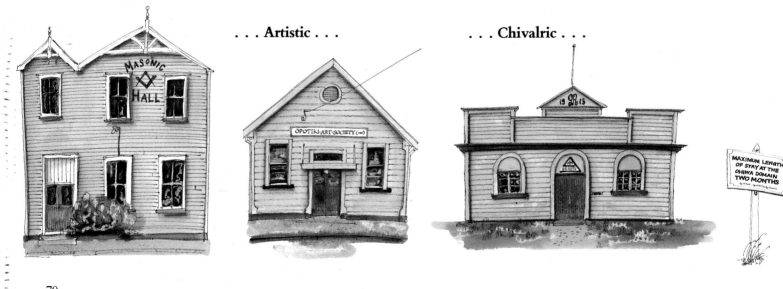

. . . Artistic . . .

. . . Chivalric . . .

70

Te Araroa. The school is named after an enormous
600-year-old pohutukawa tree growing nearby.

. . . and Methodistic.

. . . Bacchic . . .

Raukokore church, 1894.

Hicks Bay.

Raukokore.

On the road to East Cape.

East Cape.

Rotokautuku shingle plant, near Ruatoria.

Old East Cape school house.

Tokomaru Bay wharf.

Tolaga Bay.

Tolaga Bay.

Tolaga Bay.

Tolaga Bay jetty.

81

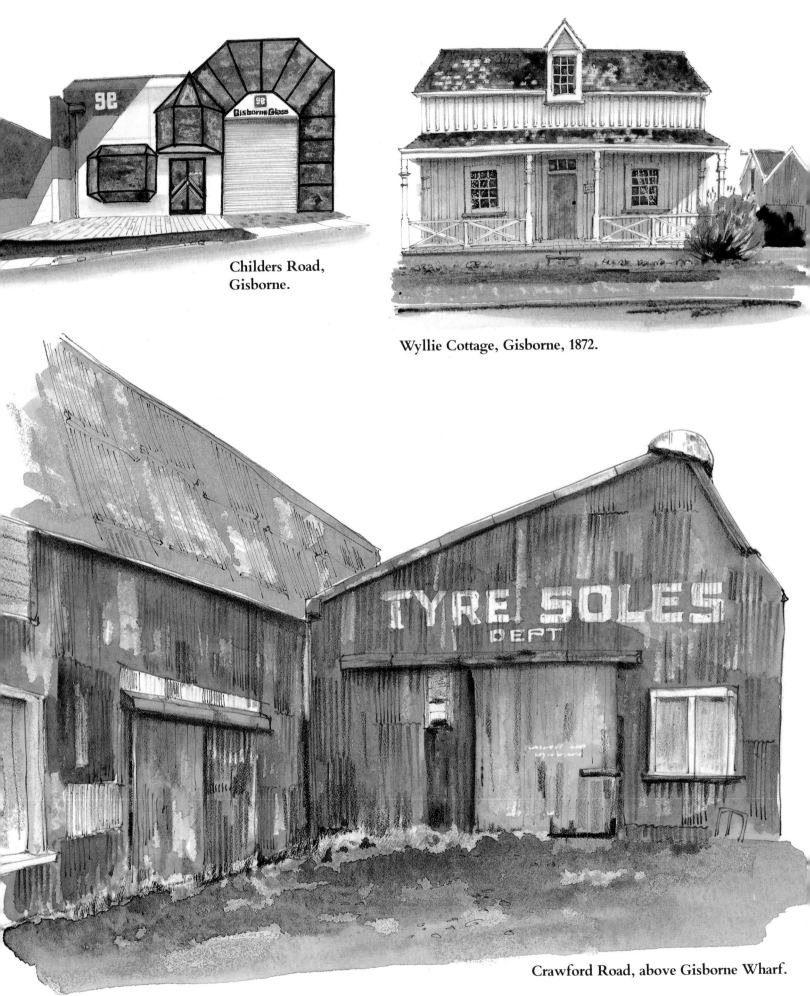

Childers Road,
Gisborne.

Wyllie Cottage, Gisborne, 1872.

Crawford Road, above Gisborne Wharf.

Gisborne fire station.

Holy Trinity, Derby Street, Gisborne. Now the parish hall, it was the second church on the site. Much better than the third, next to which it stands.

The Kindly East

HAWKE'S BAY, WAIRARAPA

In 1843, a British general, having won the Battle of Hyderabad in the province of Sind, triumphantly sent a dispatch consisting of one word, 'Peccavi'. As all good Catholics know, this translates as 'I have sinned'.

For some silly reason this fragment of history has stuck in my mind since I was a small boy. It's the sort of snippet that pays off when playing 'Trivial Pursuit'.

The reason I mention it here is that the general who sent that masterpiece of brevity and wit was Charles Napier after whom the city is named.

From the distance of 140 odd years, when New Zealand is at last more concerned with its place in the Pacific than its attachments to Great Britain, the naming of some of our towns and cities after obscure British Blimps seems bizarre, but it does serve to remind us of the European side to our origins.

Napier is famous for its 1931 earthquake whose benefit was the sudden addition of a large amount of real estate from which the local government could derive taxes. I have checked a number of references,

none of which agree as to how much land emerged. Dollimore's Guide says 7 500 acres, Mobil's Guide converts to 8 260 acres, Shadbolt's Shell Guide rounds it off at 8 000 acres and Brathwaite's Companion Guide tops the stakes with 'ten thousand acres of land'. Well, at least they weren't copying each other!

Following the earthquake, devastation being so extensive, the opportunity was taken, in a rare exhibition of civic unanimity, to rebuild the city along an integrated design scheme. Napier, consequently and uniquely in New Zealand, has many outstanding art deco buildings, which, in the 1980s, have safely arrived at a point of architectural preservation — they are classics.

It's always been surprising to me that Hastings and Napier, only 20 kilometres apart, have managed to remain discrete and determinedly so. They even manage to have their own separate, daily newspapers — organs whose titles smack of power politics and commerce on a global scale — the Napier *Daily Telegraph* and the *Hawke's Bay Herald-Tribune*.

I discovered to my delight that Hastings — which honours some obscure Governor-General of the East India Company — was almost named after the chap who laid out the town: Francis Hicks. I wonder what effect a simple difference in name might have had upon the psyches of the inhabitants? How profound might be the burden of being a citizen of Hicksville?

Regrettably, for the whole of Hawke's Bay area is rich and pleasant, there was a paucity of material for this book, with Napier providing infinitely more than Hastings.

I've often heard it said that Australia, especially Sydney and Melbourne, is so colourful and exciting, culturally, because of the variety of the ethnic origins of immigrants who have settled over the years. The comparison is made with New Zealand, less venturesome and so rather dull — especially in the areas of dining-out, theatre, art, and its development as a polyglot nation. Yet, in the past, attempts have been made to introduce a wider range of nationalities. I call two to mind. In the north Auckland region, at Puhoi, a Bohemian settlement was set up in 1863. The poor Slavs arrived to find they'd been sold steep scrub and bush hillsides, which they had to clear to make the farmland to which they'd thought they were coming. In Puhoi you'll still hear fractured English spoken!

The other settlement is in the Dannevirke/Norsewood vicinity to which Scandinavians from Norway, Denmark and Sweden were imported with the intention of carving pasture from bush and cutting the road that is now State Highway 2 through from the northern Wairarapa to Hawke's Bay.

Marine Parade, Napier.
Each house is fundamentally the same yet each studiously contrives to be distinctive.

There's nothing obvious in Dannevirke to connect it with its origins, but Norsewood has a little more to offer. It's an interesting spot, split in two by the highway, leaving Upper Norsewood to the west and Lower Norsewood to the east of the road, the two connected by a viaduct. Like the Scots of Dunedin, who are more Scottish than the Scots, one suspects that the Scandinavians of Norsewood cleave over-passionately to their misty origins.

When I visited I heard no fractured English, in fact I heard nothing for I hardly saw a soul, and those I saw looked at me as though I were from the moon. Perhaps that bisecting main highway is so attractive to the foot-down motorist that the Norsewoods are condemned to a tourism passover?

It's the same empty ocean that washes the wanton walls of the Wairarapa as provides the moat between East Cape and Chile. But one is not so constantly aware of the sea. If it is to be seen from the Wairarapa, a deliberate excursion must be made to the coast from the main road, to places like Porangahau, Castlepoint or Riversdale.

The utter charm of the Wairarapa lies in the series of earnest little towns that are strung out like beads on a necklace from the Manawatu Gorge to the foot of the Rimutakas. From the road, the eye is constantly drawn west to the forested Tararua mountains from which flow the rivers that lace Wairarapa's alluvial plain, leaving, as in Canterbury, paddocks of stones to blunt the plough.

The main road lies closer to the mountains than the sea. It's no coincidence that in doing so there is a straighter line drawn between Wellington and Hawke's Bay.

Whether by oversight, love or accident, a rich leaving of colonial cottages and settler buildings still exists in the towns that serve the farmlands. In Woodville, Mangatainoka (what a brewery!), Pahiatua (that ugly Harvard!), Eketahuna, Masterton, Carterton, Greytown and Featherston you'll find remaining specimens of country cottages, many of which have caught the attention of Wellingtonians and are up for restoration — no expense spared.

The wonder of it is that the restorations are good, restrained and contriving to care for the outline while still providing those tired treasury officers with their creature comforts.

Napier waterfront.

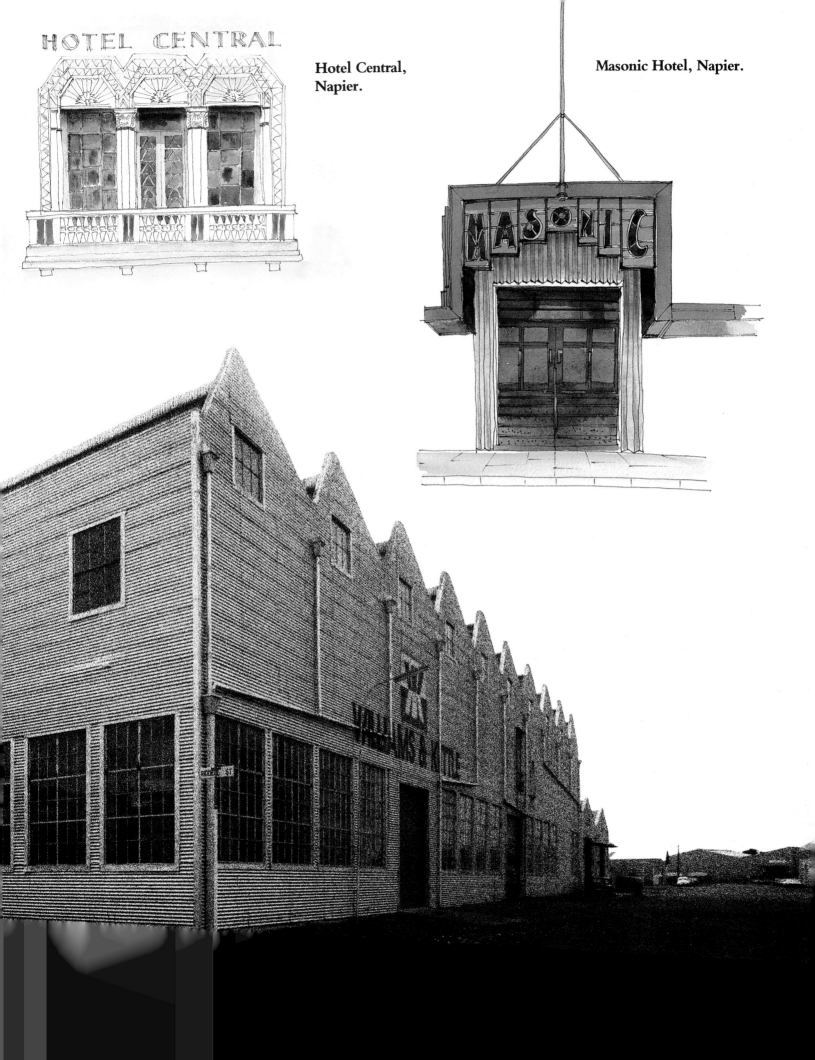

Hotel Central,
Napier.

Masonic Hotel, Napier.

Near Pakipaki.

Athfield architecture, Havelock North.

Sacred Heart, Hastings.

Old flour mill,
Carterton.

Pahiatua.

DISTRICT
JAIL
1884 - 1930 PRESENT
SITE 1935

Upper Norsewood.

Masterton.

TRANSPORT WAIRARAPA Ltd.

Daily Services

CARTERTON
GREYTOWN

AUCKLAND-WELLINGTON

FEATHERSTON
MARTINBOROUGH

MAILS RAIL & TOWN
DELIVERY

Mangatainoka.

Eketahuna.

91

Greytown — such elderly ladies!

Featherston.

Greytown.

South-west Quadrant

KING COUNTRY, TARANAKI, CENTRAL DESERT, MANAWATU, WELLINGTON

Land wars to its north and in Taranaki to the south left the King Country very much as it is today — a tough nut to crack. It's little wonder that Maori guerillas of the Waikato sought security in the lands of the Ngati Maniapoto, for even today the terrain is tortuous, demanding full attention from the motorist, whose whole time is spent changing gears and negotiating bends.

King Tawhiao's adoption of the Ngati Maniapoto's forests and hills led to its modern name. From the crumpled hills, disapprobation of Pakeha ways radiated like waves, and it wasn't until early this century, when the railway lines from the Waikato and Wellington had joined, that King Country finally became peacefully accessible to Europeans.

It's not just the King Country that's rough. The whole topographical model from Te Kuiti to Wanganui and from Ahitihi to Ohakune looks, from the air, like a piece of greenish paper that God has screwed into a ball then tried to flatten out again.

Mt Egmont completely dominates the Taranaki area. Photographers attempting, on behalf of some primary producer's export effort, to cram the whole of New Zealand into one brilliant colour shot have many times dished up the old cliché — Mt Egmont (the Fujiyama of the South Pacific), snow-capped in a clear, blue sky, with lush green dairy pastures grazed by Jerseys and full-fleeced sheep in the foreground. In the middle distance is the farmhouse, a red-roofed, double-bayed, end-of-the-century villa. All of this is overseen by the farmer mounted on a chestnut hack. It's not untruthful but it takes a lot of organisation!

Down State Highway 3 from New Plymouth to Hawera there's a series of self-important little towns that are rewarding for the artist and photographer even though they have faded from the full flush of earlier glory. Everywhere you go in the Taranaki district you'll find disused dairy factories, relics of the time when small was beautiful — and affluent. Now the micro-parochialisms have agglomerated into provincial parochialism. It's the way the world goes, from local to regional to national then multi-national. One hopes against hope that the process will repeat itself!

New Plymouth was, of course, named after the same Plymouth whence the Pilgrim Fathers set out, with high hopes, for the New World in the *Mayflower* in 1620.

Hope distinguishes the district — agricultural and dairying hope, automotive production hope, natural gas and oil hope. On occasions the surroundings are flush with wealth and success. The 'Think Big' mentality and the absolute certainty that the world's oil was disappearing fast and booming in price led to the belief that Taranaki would be as rich as the Gulf sultans because of the oil lying in its glistering strata. This has not proved to be the case; but I have a sneaking feeling that 'Think Big' will yet have its day — it's just that it will be a different day from the one expected.

Pylons on the march between the Desert Road and the view!

Army Museum, Waiouru.

Kapuni, like the Kinleith Mill in the eastern Waikato, throbs, but gently, neatly surrounded by those emerald pastures that turn the Japanese on. In itself, Kapuni is not so big; in fact it's quite discreet and proves that you don't have to destroy the landscape to exploit the earth's riches.

Out from Stratford on State Highway 43 sleeps Whangamomona. It's like many other New Zealand Brigadoons but it's unexpected. When I first 'discovered' it, it was very much more original than it is now, although one must be careful to distinguish between 'real' faded and 'filmset' faded. So many of these 'original' towns have been found and made to look even more genuine by television commercial producers and also by the extremely talented New Zealand film industry, which flourished up to the mid-eighties through generous tax concessions available to the angels. I think what we found at Whangamomona is genuine, but I'm still not quite sure . . .

Away on the other side of the Matemateaonga Range is a magical land that starts at Raetihi and finishes at Wanganui. Raetihi is host to an imposing Ratana church, which stands like a fortress, enigmatic on a hill. From Raetihi a dusty, winding track leads through sultry bush to the Wanganui River at Pipiriki and past this steep and confined settlement the big, brown river carves its course to the sea 90 kilometres away.

Like all big navigable rivers of the world, the Wanganui has affected everything through which it flows. All the villages are on the river — which makes good sense, for who would have needed highways when a river would do?

What endears me to this valley is the way in which the locals converted the names applied to the towns by an insistent missionary from English to Maori. 'We'll call this one Athens, this Corinth, another London and this one Jerusalem,' he decided. 'Thanks very much,' said the local yokels. 'As they're difficult for us to get our tongues around, we'll call them Atene, Koriniti, Ranana and Hiruharama!' (If only they'd done the same to Mt Egmont we wouldn't have this silly business about whether or not it should be called Mt Taranaki.)

The valley of the Wanganui ought to be a pleasant place to live, although nowadays both the river and the road must come under heavy tourist traffic, at times shattering the bush music so kindly provided by bellbirds and tuis — in the liquid tintinnabulation section — and overlaid by lyrical, high woodwind from the fantails and grey warblers.

The openness of its river estuary gives Wanganui breadth and a feeling of generosity. It, like Gisborne, has a look of mature comfort, a Victorian air, although I believe its fortunes have sagged lately despite its being home to that sinister 'big brother' installation the Wanganui computer.

The road to Wellington, passing Ratana — a world apart from our everyday — soon joins up at Bulls with that which comes off the central 'desert', State Highway 1.

Waiouru.

Colour, topography and mood are the attractions of the road that hugs the eastern shores of Lake Taupo. Around the southern shores of the lake, Maori and European settlements have taken advantage of thermal effusions bordering a reedy strand. Latterly activity has included the here-today-gone-tomorrow upheaval of hydro-electric exploitation.

The wasteland of the so-called desert is tailor-made for oil painters, who, unlike most first-time visitors, may ignore those pylons marching across the landscape between the main road and the mountains like outpourings of H. G. Wells's imagination.

The Army is provided with a wonderful playground in this wilderness and provides, in turn, an impressive museum — secretive and introverted from the outside — designed most sympathetically by Miles Warren.

As on the National Park road, one is impressed by the slender viaducts that pop into view, carrying the Main Trunk railway line over deep cleft gorges. Gradients had to have careful consideration when laying the line, for railway locomotives have none of the dynamic flexibility of the motor car.

And so the country opens up to the sunny dairying paddocks that typify the Marton, Bulls, Feilding, Palmerston North, Foxton and Levin flatlands. Easy country, low horizons, the occasional flash of an outdated jet fighter heading for Ohakea or the eternal kahu quartering the berms in search of carrion.

Soon the ribbon development begins, towns start to join up, a suburban look emerges. Make the effort to turn off at Paekakariki and you'll see, from the hilltop, north along the golden coast, a sight that will take your breath away before you plunge down the winding road to the Hutts and institutional Wellington.

The capital's strength is its awkward topography. Being jammed into itself by high hills on one side and the sea on the other it has all the visual pleasance of a Cornish fishing village, with some well-considered architecture to prove its importance.

Ratana church, Raetihi.

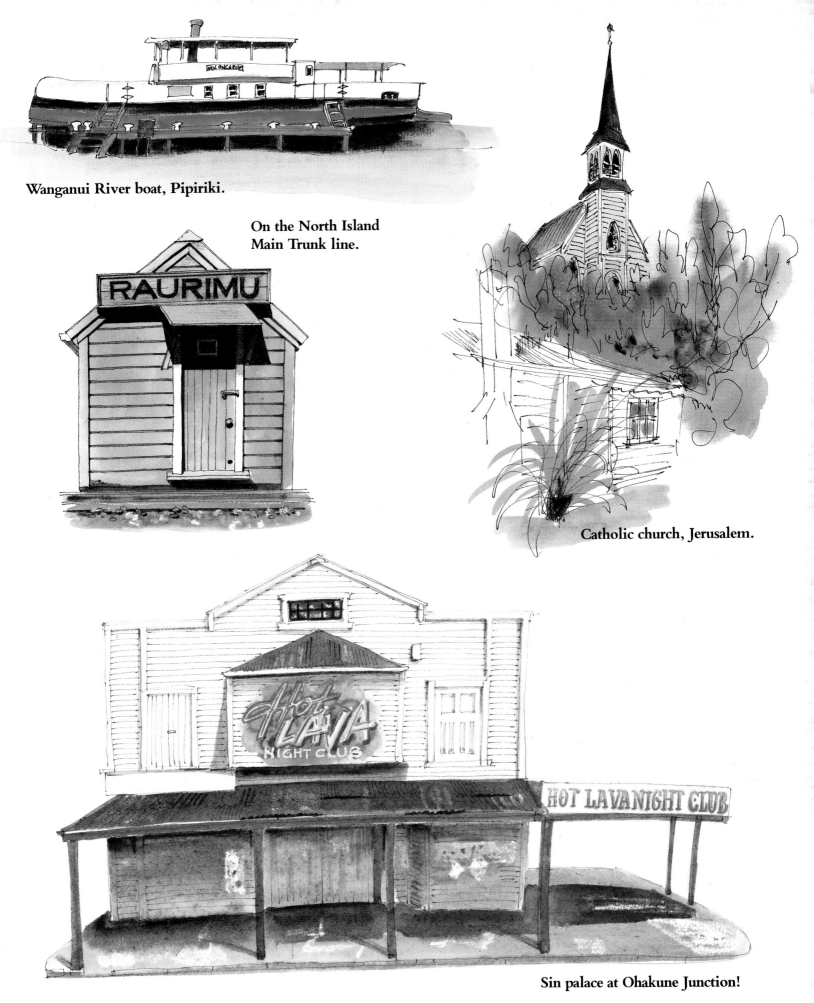

Wanganui River boat, Pipiriki.

On the North Island
Main Trunk line.

Catholic church, Jerusalem.

Sin palace at Ohakune Junction!

99

Taumarunui track and town.

Industry near Taumarunui . . .

Motutere.
What do they do in there?

Skin Jeans's tradesman's entrance, Taumarunui.

. . . and idleness at Piriaka.

Cape Egmont.

Eltham cinema.

Kapuni-in-the-fields.

King George V Coronation rotunda,
Inglewood.

Foxglove Cottage, 50 Dawson Street, New Plymouth.

On the road to Whangamomona.

Rutland Hotel, Wanganui.

DOUGLAS
BOARDING
HOUSE

Hawera.

HAWERA HANDYMAN BARN

Whangamomona.

Monument to a prosperous apothecary, Wanganui.

War memorial, Durie Hill.

Wanganui Rowing Club, Taupo Quay.

Cosmopolitan Club, Wanganui.

Marton.

Marton — a rewarding detour off the main highway.

The original Ratana temple; a seat of distinctiveness in a unique town.

Water tower in the garden
of Lethenty House, Bulls.

Local wit, New Plymouth.

The heart of the Rangitikei.

Mangaweka — the old main road. The buildings are genuine but suffered a facelift for a movie set.

A hopelessly inadequate
rendering of the UDC
Tower on Wellington's
Terrace! Reflections include
Westpac, BNZ, and ANZ
banks.

110

BNZ Tower,
Wellington.

Ian Athfield's Skyline building, Kelburn.

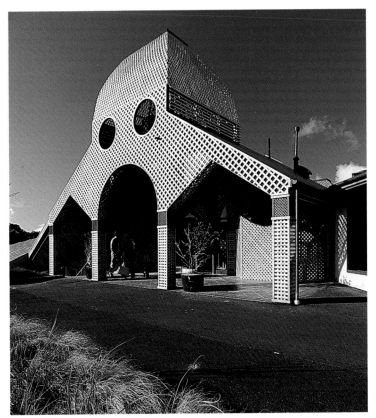

The Terrace, Wellington.

Erstwhile University Grants Committee building, Bowen Street, Wellington.

Port Nicholson tug, *Kupe*.

Oriental Parade, Wellington.

Ram's head carving by Clare Athfield,
Crown House, The Terrace.
The search for detail pays rich rewards!

Extraordinary architecture at 19 Sydney Street East,
Wellington.

More Athfield, Majoribanks Street, Wellington.

Parliament's favourite fish shop, Molesworth Street.

4 Port Street, Wellington. Urban dhobi.

6 and 8 Brougham Street, Wellington.

Motorists leaving for the South Island by Cook Strait ferry may puzzle over this — especially if they are visitors to New Zealand. Is it pejorative? Exhortative? Or the remains of a poster advertising a concert given by Engelbert Humperdinck?

Farewell North Island . . .

Tobacco, Hops
and a Marble Mountain

NELSON, MARLBOROUGH

At the time of our crossing, the ferries that plied Cook Strait were vehicles from which to look out, for to look inwards was to experience a numbing dullness that only a take-it-or-leave-it monopolist could have devised. But the view from the salt-encrusted lounge windows or breezy decks compensated amply, especially as the ferry pierced the apparently impregnable wall of the Marlborough Sounds and entered, through Tory Channel, the peaceful waters of Queen Charlotte Sound.

Picton has an air of expectancy. It is a place of arrival and departure, trains to and from the south, ferries to and from the north. Yachties and owners of distant baches load boxes of groceries — and more essential supplies — from car boot to boat, and even the odd float-plane buzzes fussily, carrying a cargo of passengers with more money than time to spare.

Just a short way south, where the crowding, gorse-yellowed hills give way to wider fields, lies Koromiko and its 'airport' (indispensable for those who still cannot face the ferry journey to Wellington). Here, too, is one of the pink-bricked buildings that turn up again and again in this region.

Once out of these northern hills over the Wairau River and through busy Blenheim, the landscape dries to soft, dun-coloured hills that look like camels' humps. The road snakes over and around them, past the crisp, marmoreal heaps of the Grassmere salt works to the coast, where, quite suddenly, the hills are replaced by steeper, craggier outcroppings of the Kaikoura Ranges.

Here, road, rail and stony beach share a narrow ledge above an impatient sea. Occasionally there is no ledge, so constricted tunnels with dripping roofs punch tiny holes in the uncompromising bluffs.

For the exhausted yachtsman there is little shelter between Cape Campbell and Motunau Island except for the peninsula of Kaikoura. This neb of land, sticking out into the restless sea like a coat peg, accommodates a worthy town, a sturdy town, Crayfishtown no less today than when it was jealously fought over by successive Maori tribes.

Miles away to the north-west, across those grand mountains and the expansive sheep and cattle country that surrounds Molesworth Station, brood the glacial Nelson lakes, Rotoroa and Rotoiti.

It was at the Lake Rotoroa lodge that Euan and I arrived in the driving rain. The ancient VW Camper was leaking like a sieve, and since it was no place to sleep we begged a bed for the night. The evening was spent around the mellow, Victorian bar, swearing entente with two visiting Americans, there for the fishing.

Next morning it was still sheeting down while those impatient Isaac Waltons played a tense game of gin rummy. As we left we heard one say, in that thoroughly relaxed drawl they all seem to have, 'If this goddamn rain don't let up soon, either you'll have a hardware store or I'll own your chain of jewellers!'

It's around here that the rocks take on that 'gold in them thar hills' look. Down the westward sides of the St Arnaud Range and the Spencer Mountains; up along the Victoria Range and through the cluttered valleys from Springs Junction; up the Maruia to Murchison and the Buller River there was gold.

Indeed, there's still gold. I've seen it as colours in gravels swirling in a camper's frying pan.

I've always had a soft spot for Murchison (or 'Murch' as the locals call it), enclosed by hills at the confluence of the Buller and Matakitaki Rivers. It was hit hard by earthquake in 1929, and it would seem, listening to parish legends, that under every house-sized rock perched on the khaki hillsides there lies, squashed, a man, his dog and his sandwiches.

Here they manufacture history while looking you straight in the eye. If you're ever in the vicinity ask them about George Fairweather Moonlight or the lost tribe of Maori.

The importance of Route 6 is its connection of Nelson and the West Coast. It's a historic road and was carved arduously out of the adamantine rocks of the Buller. Today, it's an invigorating drive from one end to the other, but the frequent stopping places for horse-drawn traffic of the goldfields still punctuate the state highway, most of them modified and some only evident to sharp eyes, having been destroyed by fire or other accidental or deliberate means.

Once over the Hope Saddle a generous vista opens across the lower hills and plains of Motupiko, the Mouteres and Tasman Bay. As always a sight of the sea, however distant, seems to lift the spirits.

The road to Nelson through Belgrove, Foxhill, Wakefield, Brightwater and Richmond was a glory for Euan and me for on either side, for mile after mile lay weathered derelict houses, preserved colonial relics, railway memorabilia and the recurrent pleasure of old post offices.

We discovered, in Nelson, the work of a highly amusing *trompe-l'oeil* artist whom the local authorities have not stopped from painting the most intriguing murals. We were particularly taken with — and envious of — the 'open window' painting that has much improved the old electricity building. The same artist might be employed to make the chief post office look like a rocket launcher instead of just playing at it!

Joking aside, Nelson is a noble city full of attractive homes and buildings, well cared for. And on a calm morning the prospect across Tasman Bay from the Blenheim road is positively tranquillising.

Though dotted all over with huts and relics, the Marlborough Sounds, with the exception of Rai Valley, Pelorus Bridge, Havelock and other settlements at the base of the Sounds, did not lure us. The Sounds are more for geologists than artists (although I remember once sketching on D'Urville Island with some affection).

New Zealand's standard farming images are sheep, cattle and cereal crops, which, after a while, can become tedious. In the Nelson area there is a welcome difference. Orcharding, tobacco and hops are more interesting; and worm farming is positively kinky! The practical attractiveness of hop kilns immediately activates the shutter finger and makes the palm of the painting hand itch.

Tobacco kilns have the same effect. In the eternal sun that blesses this region, they have an established look of usefulness, and inside their timbers have absorbed the aromas of years to give off, in the cool darkness, reassuring perfumes. Here in the fields where hops grow on strings and broad, verdant tobacco leaves give up their fortune to chattering Martian machines that trundle the corded windrows, there's a delicious warmth; moist, luxurious, fecund. Clearly the Motueka valley is kind to its tillers.

Ngarua Limeworks, part way over Takaka Hill, the marble mountain, has some shapely quarry buildings. We wanted to look at them and asked permission of the manager. Before agreeing, he scrutinised us suspiciously through dust-covered eyebrows and asked if we were 'greenies'!

. . . Hello, Picton.

Takaka's about as far from anywhere as anywhere but Euan's face was known to the girl in the general store where we stopped to buy groceries. 'I know you,' she said.

Euan gulped.

'You did the photographs for my sister's wedding in Christchurch.'

He relaxed.

It's a one-way street past lonely Collingwood, past the marching stumps of a long-decaying jetty pointing across the mud-flats of Golden Bay to the veiled hills of Ligar Bay. South of the enchantments of Whanganui Inlet — a bowl of porridge surrounded by limestone outcrops — we found a rural school where we stopped to get water and enjoy one of the many cups of tea we brewed on the VW's stove. The children came out to play. Strange, unusually beautiful children like beings from another planet, they skipped across the damp grass bare-footed, collecting mushrooms, which they brought us as gifts.

And as soon as they'd come, they'd gone.

Not far beyond, the road ends.

Picton.

Picton's waterfront watering hole.

122

Koromiko airport terminal.

Freeth's old wine room, Koromiko.

St Mary's, Blenheim.

Blenheim.

St Mary's Presbytery, 61 Maxwell Road.

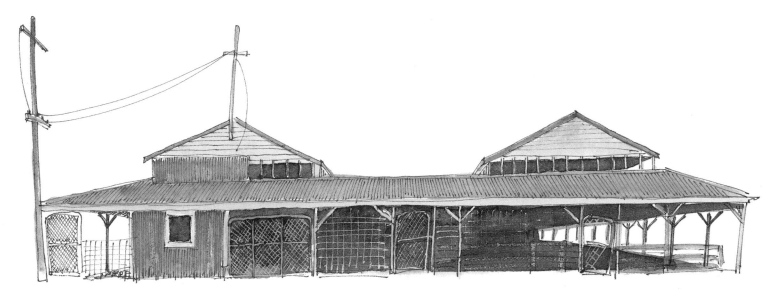

Stockyards, Marlborough A&P Showgrounds.

Malthouse, Riverlands.

Pomposity for the posthumous, Blenheim.

Blenheim.

They say that the plans for a church were mixed up
with those for the post office. Makes a good story . . .

Riverlands.

Nelson.

On Tasman Bay.

Protected by a naturally formed breakwater of boulders, Nelson Haven, at times, is simply another way of saying tranquillity.

Baptist church, Nelson.

Trafalgar Street.

Inglis Hops kiln, Riwaka.

Tobacco crop, Brooklyn Farm, Motueka.

Helminthic husbandry in Brooklyn Valley.

Upper Takaka — west of the Marble Mountain.

The silversmith's house, Whanganui Inlet.

Inside of a Bendix washing machine, Pakawau.

'Fairholme', East Takaka Road.

Whanganui Inlet: 'a bowl of porridge'.

1887 Tophouse hostelry, scene of a murder in 1894, now in private ownership.

Tophouse mailbox.

Old Longford store.

Bush hut near St Arnaud.

Derelict Glenhope Railway Station, southern terminus
of the old line from Nelson.

Murchison.

St George's, Motupiko.

The front door of the old
Uruwhenua school house.

Belgrove Railway
Station windmill, 1898.

139

Reid's store, Maruia.

Kaikoura.

Reid's store, Maruia.

Southern Comfort

CANTERBURY

Like an amphitheatre, the mountains and their foothills sweep around from Lowry Peaks in the north, through the Crawford Range and the long bulk of the Southern Alps, to curve south and south-east through the Tom Thumb Range and the Hunters Hills to the Waitaki River mouth.

These lofty tiers and terraces gaze over limestone downs to the ultimate alluvial plains — formed of their own disintegration — and ponder on the anomaly of Banks Peninsula.

This plum pudding of an ex-island separates Pegasus Bay from the Canterbury Bight. In so doing it not only provides an underused playground for Christchurch but also acts as a crushing device, turning the semi-precious beach stones of Birdlings Flat into fine sand as the northerly press of ocean current drives alluvium around the tooth-like promontories of the peninsula to the long shallow beaches — New Brighton, Kairaki, Woodend, Waikuku and Amberley.

All New Zealanders, before they die, should go to Banks Peninsula. It is a glorious district, much much bigger than expected, laced by roads, tracks and stock routes, which evidence much activity in the past, and sprinkled with farm settlements full of character and distinction, whether they border the flooded craters of Lyttelton or Akaroa, or the deeply indented outer bays.

Over many years practically all of the bays and many of the hillsides have heard the scratch of my drawing pen or the click of Euan's shutter; and the

Antigua Boat Sheds, Avon River, 1882.

142

wheeze of an old air-cooled flat-four VW motor is not unfamiliar to the philosophical sheep that tour these friendly hills.

Things tend to last in Canterbury; not just in a physical sense, but historically or dynastically. This is the land of the big sheep runs and famous stations that took on the uncompromising might of the alpine range and won. Typically, their headquarters lie high up under the peaks, and their owners, whatever their generation, respect and honour the cradle of their heritage. I remember being astonished, on entering the lounge of one homestead many years ago, to read, carved on the pelmet of the large window in old English letters, 'I will lift up mine eyes unto the hills from whence cometh my strength'. It would have been crass had it not been so humbly true.

Christchurch is a magnet to these outlander farmers. It is to this old city with its English atmosphere that they come to stock up on tweeds and twin sets or to take tea with sons or daughters at school or university. It's a city that indulgently encourages some of the best of modern New Zealand architecture while proudly paying compliments to stately old edifices with well-tended lawns, parks and a cherished Avon whose trout have little to fear provided they stay within sight of the town bridges.

Canterbury is a province of extreme contrasts. Down on the plains, with their quiet, nice little towns, each with its stock and station agency, the impressions are of comfort, dryness, flatness; sheep, cash crops and low horizons. The roads run straight to the edge of the sky and the view is only broken from time to time by belts of firs, macrocarpa or poplars, without which the fragile topsoil would be whipped off the land by marauding nor'westers and carried out to sea.

North of the Ashley River lies the first contrast. Rolling hills and meandering streams confine the views to a series of cameos where, even now, the remains of

old cob cottages are quite common. Around Weka Pass, on the way to the winter resort of Hanmer, the limestone is at its best with sculptured outcrops calling for imagination to liken them to some human or animal form. Limestone, I'm sure, was created to please mankind. The turf always contrasts happily with the white, grey or cream of the rock where travellers, for centuries, have sheltered and whiled away the time by exercising the art of graffiti.

Miles away to the very south of this region lie similar rocks east of Burkes and Mackenzie Passes, around Fairlie, Cave and down to Waimate and the hills of Waihao.

I've heard it said (although I'm not sure of the truth of the matter) that it was once possible to get a driving licence in Christchurch for flat land. If you wanted to go up the hills you needed a more advanced qualification! That suggests limited horizons, and I'm sure there are many Cantabrians who have never left the plain or experienced another of those contrasts — the alpine and sub-alpine districts.

The contrast is amazing, and never more so than after travelling west from Christchurch, through Darfield and Springfield, climbing imperceptibly to the foot of Porters Pass. From there to the top is no more than five or ten minutes' drive, but it takes you from one world to another.

Over the pass lie lakes, mountains and rivers of unrivalled beauty and remoteness. Beyond lies the main ridge of the Southern Alps and the headwaters of those wanton streams, like the Waimakariri, whose relentless channels drain the summer snows of the spine of the South Island, waters opalescent, rumbling with the eastward tumble of riverbed boulders.

The roadbuilders of the Canterbury Plains must have had an easy, if boring, task in comparison with those of the central North Island. From Kaikoura to Waipara, over the tumbling Hundalees, life wouldn't have been easy; but south of there, past Kaiapoi and Marshlands to Christchurch and on down the plain to Glenavy it would have been a pushover.

Not that the road's watering holes are boring. Every one of those towns has much to offer the graphic recorder who's faced with the problem of what to leave out rather than scratching around for subject matter; and the inland roads like Route 7 to the Lewis Pass, or that pretty alternative to State Highway 1, Route 72, are just as rewarding. This particular road delimits the Canterbury Plains and their western foothills. It runs faithfully at the border

and so passes through some of the best small towns Canterbury can offer — Oxford, Coalgate, Windwhistle, Alford Forest, Mayfield and sweet Geraldine — a garden of Eden!

Timaru and Napier have one thing in common for me; they remind me of English seaside towns for they each have a 'front' — a promenade area devoted to the pleasures of day-trippers and holiday-makers. Caroline Bay, the seaside area overlooked by Timaru, fills up at Christmas and the 'goings on' on New Year's Eve usually rate a mention in the *Timaru Herald* or even the Christchurch *Press*. One suspects that even if Caroline Bay were empty on 31 December unspeakable acts performed there would still rate a few centimetres in the newspapers — tradition is so important to a reputation.

I was told when I arrived in 1960 that I would find a little of England in Canterbury. It's truer now than it was then but only because English time has been preserved here; in England it has moved on and is no longer recognisable.

The Red Post. In 1988, somebody painted it yellow! I hope it is now red again!

Red Post Junction near Culverden. The post has marked the proposed junction of two railways since 1873.

Leithfield.

Mt Grey.

Kaiapoi.

Ohoka, circa 1870, near Rangiora.

Hurunui Hotel, built of North Canterbury limestone in 1869.

Kaiapoi rail yards.

Cathedral of the Blessed
Sacrament, Christchurch.

Christchurch College Chapel.

Christchurch mosque.

Canterbury Provincial Buildings.

Cashel Street, Christchurch.

FAIL'S CAFE

FAIL'S CAFE

Zealand's Oldest Seafood Restaurant

NAVAL ASSN.

KEEP CLEAR

Old Union Rowing Club, Avonside.

**Wordsworth Street,
Sydenham.**

153

Victoria Street.

Synagogue, Gloucester Street, Christchurch.

Pegasus Press, 14 Oxford Terrace.

At Christchurch Boys High School.

Lancaster Park, Christchurch.

River Road pumphouse.

Sydenham Park.

Ferry Road pumping station.

Blackheath Place, Durham Street, Christchurch.

Heathcote.

Victoria Street, Christchurch.

Riccarton Road,
Christchurch.

88 Hereford Street, Christchurch.

Governors Bay jetty, Lyttelton Harbour.

Cass Bay clarity . . .

. . . Christchurch smog.

159

St Cuthbert's, Governors Bay.

160

Captain Simeon's house, Lyttelton, 1852.

Banks Peninsula Cruising Club.

Lyttelton. Site of New Zealand's first telegraph.

Canterbury Street, Lyttelton.

Okains Bay, Banks Peninsula.

Brookshaw woolshed, Pigeon Bay.

Okains Bay library.

The little red school bus,
Allandale.

Brookshaw woolshed
(photographic detail).

The Kaik, Onuku Marae, Akaroa.

Akaroa.

Church Street, Akaroa. Old shipping
office built entirely of wood.

St Patrick's, Akaroa, 1864.

ELLESMERE BRASS BAND

Leeston.

Geraldine.

GERALDINE GARDEN CENTRE

BAA LIVE SHEEP EXPORTS

Modified protest, Winslow, Canterbury.

Waihao Downs.

Mailbox, Old West Coast Road, Yaldhurst.

Holy Child, Ashburton.

Timaru lighthouse, 1878. It now stands inland.

Between High and Grigson Streets, Waimate.

Two-man army huts at West Melton.

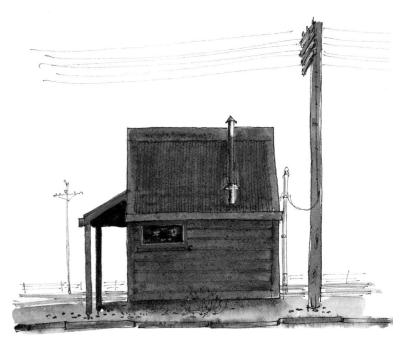

New Zealand Railways architecture at St Andrews.

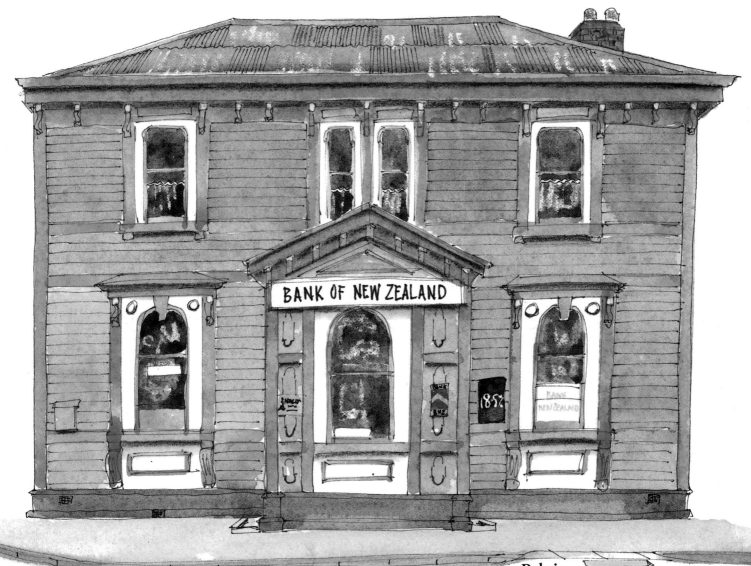

BANK OF NEW ZEALAND

Rakaia.

Evans Atlas flour mill. Timaru, 1888.

On Main South Road near Waimate.

Whispering Tussock, Flattened Trees

OTAGO, SOUTHLAND

Central Otago is like a recurrent disease; a malaria. It causes itches that must be scratched. Once bitten the brain becomes its slave. For ever afterwards it must be revisited.

The ghosts are not remote or ill-defined as those of Northland. They are tangible. You feel them on the sighing winds that rustle the golden-green tussock. They are present in dusty corners of derelict roadhouses. They stand ready to repossess and reuse the silent rusting gold-mining machinery that lies, discarded, across this historic land.

So intensively were the terraces and gullies of Central endowed with gold that townships grew and died overnight in close proximity to each other. Many remain, for after the gold hunger was sated there were other, more permanent riches to be garnered.

Our favourite entry from the north has been down Route 8 through inland Canterbury and Mackenzie Country then over Lindis Pass with its tussock-spread hills all cuddly like soft toys.

I remember us sitting in the VW Camper at the top of the pass, drinking yet another cup of tea, only a

Ettrick.

few metres between us and the lowering cloud base, when a light aircraft passed above, going north, heading home, for daylight was almost ended. We watched in awe as the craft jinked and swung, following the serpentine pass road in the narrow stratum of clear air below the seal-grey cloud, until it disappeared around a corner, well on the way to Canterbury. A late-running farmer? Who knows, but he'd done it before and he did it very well.

There are many other ways into Central. The Pigroot from Palmerston or the more secret and exciting Danseys Pass from the back of Oamaru will both take you to old gold — Naseby, Kyeburn, Ranfurly and haunted St Bathans, where you may, if you have a will, clearly hear the click of billiard balls and hoots of sudden laughter from full bearded faces above pink flannel chests.

To extract full value, exploiters of Otago have had to fight every inch of the way, for those stern rocks do not give up their treasures lightly. Look at the roads through Skippers Gorge or over the Crown Range. Wonder at the dams of the Waitaki at Aviemore and Benmore, or those of the Clutha at Roxburgh or pendent Clyde. Think of the hopeful miner plodding across the terrible Old Dunstan Road over the merciless Rock and Pillar Range, perhaps to die huddled against furious, icy rain.

Now it's all so cosy as the tour buses and aircraft pour visitors into sophisticated Queenstown and the slopes of Coronet Peak.

Down south or out at the coast there's less drama, but the views are superb. Oamaru, first town below the Waitaki River, blessed with many buildings of Oamaru stone — like shortbread, almost edible — starts a coast road to Dunedin. An untroubled road, passing Moeraki where some long-forgotten giant left his gallstones on the beach, on the way to that dour Caledonian city laden with architectural gems.

There's plenty of masonry in Dunedin; in fact, in the whole of Otago and Southland. They built to last here, using local materials — limestone from Oamaru and the ubiquitous schist, layered and sparkling like fool's gold.

177

The hills of Otago Peninsula are greener than Banks Peninsula but no less steep and encrusted with as many architectural jewels. It's a more heavily residential area, and Otago Harbour, deeply penetrating the surrounding hills, makes a fine scene through any picture window.

The Taieri Plain, being the only flat land near Dunedin, not only gives good grazing to dairy herds but also preserves an astonishing number of gracious old homes. They are manifestations of past prosperity and the determination of their founders to stay for good in this once distant colony. Moving from one to another, one gains an impression that some of the erstwhile neighbours of the plain may not have been above trying to outdo each other. There is a marked lack of modesty in some of the houses that present the grand façades of the gentry.

On south past woollen mills, bonny Balclutha and the bricks of Benhar, gentler roads lead to Central Otago or to Southland, but the prettiest and least used is the Catlins Forest road around the coast and over the hills, enchanting in the season of the year when clematis garlands the bush.

Flat Invercargill hides its occupants. On a Saturday morning, when all the shops are open and all the parking meters taken up in the main street, where do the people go? Perhaps it's just a matter of scale — the streets are so wide, the shops so capacious that, like a baggy suit, the town is too big for its citizens!

Way down here in the south, not far from half years of day and night, twilight sends the late sun,

tangerine, to lengthen the day and bathe the fine old buildings in a warm glow.

A short step farther south and you might, if you stand on tiptoes, just see the odd iceberg as it breaks up in the seas below Campbell Island over the loom of Stewart Island across Foveaux Strait. Then again, you might turn your face away if the wind at Bluff is as shrill and icy as when we were there. Tears etched snail-like tracks across our cheeks, our teeth hurt with the cold . . .

At the Foveaux Strait end of the Longwood Range near the seaside resort of Riverton there are pine trees that gave up trying to grow upwards right from the start. They are fully grown but — horizontal: They point inland towards the last brave villages bordering southern Fiordland, Tuatapere, Orawia, Ohai and the now sad hamlet of Nightcaps, an old coal-mining town where fewer feet walk these days, leaving mauve and yellow pansies to grow through cracks in the pavement, wasting their sweetness on the deserted air.

Away from Southland's lambs and ewes, past the Hokonui Hills, lies the road to Te Anau and Milford whose exquisite peaks have been paid ample attention in scenic tomes. It's never possible to see the sandflies in those pictures! Past that turnoff winds the road to Kingston and Queenstown, hugging Lake Wakatipu where the old ship *Earnslaw* takes tourists for a ride.

Night is falling fast, and it's time to take the puny road that so recently conquered the route through the Gates of Haast to the West Coast.

Lane's Emulsion factory.

Meek's grain elevator, Oamaru, 1883.

Oamaru Railway Station.

iterion Hotel, Oamaru, 1877. Later it was spray-painted for a movie.

National Bank, Oamaru.

Palmerston.

Usk Street, Oamaru.

180

On Blueskin Road, Port Chalmers.

ARAMOANA SAVE IT

31 Currie Street, Port Chalmers.

Port Chalmers.

181

Greenhouse, Larnach's Castle.

Pukehiki,
Otago Peninsula.

Outhouse, Larnach's Castle.

On the Portobello Road.

182

Dunedin.

Larnach's Castle, Otago Peninsula.

Cargill's Castle. Irresistible decay!

St Clair.

Dundas Street, Dunedin.

Art deco bus depot, Dunedin.

Otago Boys High School, Dunedin.
The architect was Ted McCoy.

Taiaroa Head, Otago Peninsula.

Otago Boys High.

187

St Clair.

1008 & 1014 George Street, Dunedin.

188

24 Duke Street, Dunedin.

**Hillside Road,
Dunedin.
Extinguished 1988.**

Mornington, Dunedin.

Manor Place, Dunedin.

Gordon Road, Mosgiel.

Gore.

Clairinch, 1878. Taieri Plain.

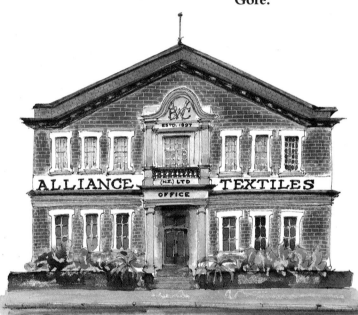

Elderlee Street, Milton.

Duddingstone, 1864. Taieri Plain.

The Poplars, 1876. MacDonald Road, Taieri Plain.

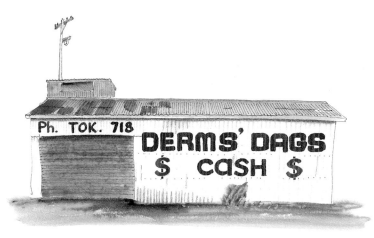

Tokanui.

Papatowai, Catlins Forest Park.

54 Mersey Street, Gore.

Coronation Library, Gore.

Bluff signal station.

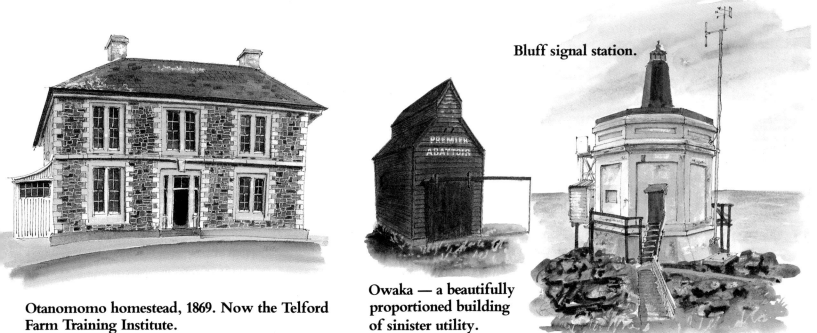

Otanomomo homestead, 1869. Now the Telford Farm Training Institute.

Owaka — a beautifully proportioned building of sinister utility.

Nightcaps Medical Association!

Nightcaps Museum.

Invercargill.

St Mary's Basilica, Invercargill.

194

Nightcaps generalists.

Nightcaps.

195

Greenhills. Anglican, Methodist
and Presbyterian co-operation.

Pines at Pahia whose only chance of
survival against the southerly winds is
to grow parallel to the ground.

Shingle Creek.

Roxburgh.

Presbyterian manse, 20 Peel Street, Lawrence.

Former Lawrence court house.

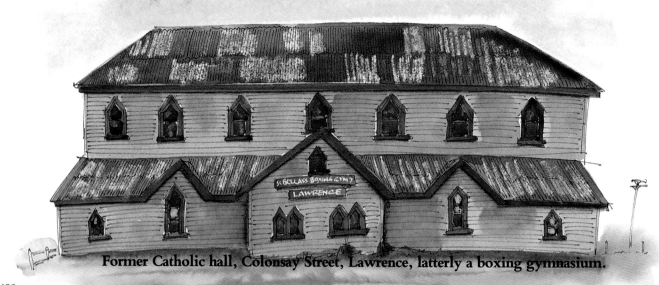

Former Catholic hall, Colonsay Street, Lawrence, latterly a boxing gymnasium.

Central Otago pastoral.

Cottesbrook wool shed
— shearers' graffiti.

Cottesbrook at Middlemarch, against the Rock and Pillar Range.

Sutton Halt.

Naseby trapezium.

201

Linnburn Station wool shed near Patearoa.

Paerau Valley, Central Otago.

Omakau.

BEWARE
OF
WIND

Lauder.

204

Near St Bathans.

Becks.

205

Clyde.

Former post office and
postmaster's house, St Bathans.

Restoration at Clyde.

St Bathans, circa 1869.

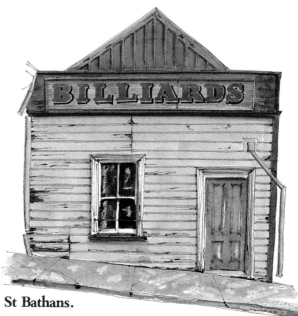

St Bathans.

Clyde.

Cromwell Gorge.

Clyde was originally called Dunstan.

Cromwell.

Old Masonic Lodge at Cromwell, a survivor of the creation of Lake Dunstan.

Antediluvian Cromwell.

Hanson's Cottage, Cromwell. First owned by G.W. Goodger, brewer, then by Murrell, 'watchmaker and tooth puller'.

Speargrass Flat.

Buckingham Street, Arrowtown.

55 Buckingham Street.

Arrow Junction.

Lodge Arrow, Killwinning No. 86.

Marine Parade, Queenstown.

New Zealand Rail depot, Queenstown wharf.

TSS *Earnslaw*, the Wakatipu steamer.

Lindis swells.

212

Cameron Flat, Haast Pass Road (Sarginson's feet!).

HUMP

Lindis humps.

Yesterday Revisited

WEST COAST

In 1860 a real estate agent functioning on a grand scale bought the West Coast for the New Zealand Government. It is, from our perspective, ironic that payment to the Maori was three hundred gold sovereigns, for the medium of his exchange was not only a principal ingredient in the soil of his purchase, it was lying around waiting to be picked up!

Less than six years later, in the first month of 1866, 19 000 and 18 250 ounces of gold were shipped out of Hokitika and Greymouth respectively.

As with Central Otago, the coast is a place you go on revisiting, for it calls all who have been once to come again. An old friend of Christchurch days, who died young, wrote the definitive work on the goldfields of the Coast. He who had achieved respect and local fame was brought back in death and lies in the windswept cemetery overlooking Ross, his birthplace. Ross typifies every goldtown on the Coast and Phil Ross May typified every Coaster; quiet, unassuming and deeply in love with the land of his birth.

Wind, salt and rain strip the paint off every building. They shape planed and dressed timbers with inexorable persistence, turning straight into undulant, rectangle into rhomboid. Wood grain opens. Steel and cast iron rust and stain the crumbling timbers. Mosses and lichens mottle the weary surfaces.

Here in Ross, or in any other town, city or village from Jackson Head to the Kohaihai River, nothing of any architectural significance whatsoever has been built in recent times. Consequently very little has been deliberately demolished. Old buildings, untenanted, quite simply die of exquisite decay, pierced through their hearts by trees, engulfed by rambling roses planted by long-gone dwellers, eaten away by insects and fungi.

Eaten away by insects! We entered the Coast by way of Haast Pass. It was late; we were tired. Soft, persistent rain had welcomed us at the Gates of Haast. We searched for accommodation, feeling too far gone to cook and sleep in the Camper. But the only motel we found, somewhere north of Haast, was tainted by

Reefton.

the tourist boom of the late eighties, greedy, overpriced and run by a surly man in need of a bath. So we parked by the beach, opened the windows no more than a centimetre, and slept.

A sharp, intolerable irritation on the point of my elbow woke me. A sandfly. My gravelled eyes focused on its friends and relations, crowding the windows, curtains, bedding, and dancing silently in the cold, damp air. Eaten away by insects! I dragged off the sleeping bag and stepped out onto the puddled parking area, down the damp bank to the beach, a creamy strand with a small stream at its northern end where I bathed hurriedly in the amontillado waters. Eaten away by insects! They followed me like a cloud, biting where skin runs tight over bone, struggling in my hair, dying from savage blows only to be replaced tenfold. We escaped them by driving quickly north, a van full of fly spray making erratic progress from that beach. Perhaps they were friends of the motel proprietor.

He could not have been a Coaster. They're too friendly. It seems the less hospitable a land the more friendly the natives. I wonder how closely any of them are related to the early miners? Australians, Californians, Irish, English, Chinese. They rushed from one rush to another, tramping north then south then north again as rumours of strikes ran like bush fires up and down the coast. They built whole towns, a pub on every corner, then walked away from them. They roamed rugged tracks in search of auriferous fortune but few prospered.

The highway is a good one now for it carries traffic on the round trip through Haast Pass, taking in the southern lakes of Otago as well as those icy flows of crumbling candle wax, the Fox and Franz Josef Glaciers, that tumble at lightning speed — for glaciers — into the dripping, sub-tropical coastal bush.

Up along this highway, out to the sea at contemplative Okarito, is the home of the sacred *Egretta alba*, the white heron or kotuku. From this, its only breeding place in New Zealand, it flaps lazily to all parts of the country, distinctive, emblematic, virginal and not at all disposed to perching sideways on your car aerial in the cocky manner of a rifleman!

Gold rushes are traumatic experiences. They inject large numbers of people into areas for short spaces of time, people who turn over the earth without thought for the future, then move on leaving an impression that the elastic of the landscape has been stretched beyond recovery. Forever afterwards there's a feeling of desertion and depopulation. One gets this feeling on the Coast, especially between Harihari and Greymouth, but north of that diluvial town, where

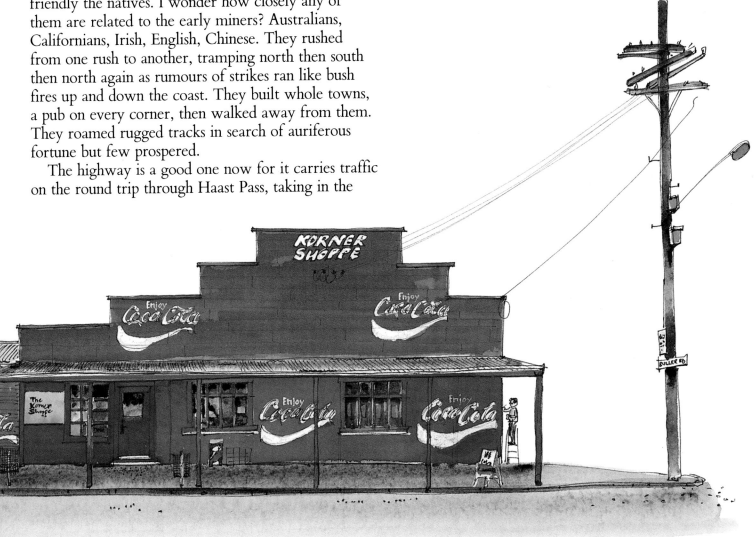

215

the steep hills of the Paparoa Range rise closely by the sea, there is less disturbance.

Looking north along this coast, particularly from Punakaiki, there's a spectacular series of headlands, pounded by the Tasman Sea, receding with diminishing clarity through the fine gauze of high-flown spray. Either side of the Paparoa Range — take your choice— it's majestic. Inland the road goes to Reefton along the Grey River valley and then to Inangahua Junction on the Buller Gorge; or by the coast past Charleston, once the site of one of the most famous pubs of all — the 'European' — to Westport.

Coal has been the second fortune of the Coast; the Paparoa Range and the hills east of Westport still yield black treasure. But to imagine what coal was like in its heyday it's necessary to take the winding road to Denniston and stand at the top of its famous incline. Today, all you'll hear is the wind, but it takes little to hear the banging, crashing, rattling thunder of gravity-driven wagons carrying coal from high in the hills, down gradients at times one-in-one to the coastal flats below.

From here north one is lured on by the knowledge that the road will come to an end. This enticement is common, I believe. In England one travels to Land's End; in global terms, to the North or South Poles; in New Zealand to Cape Reinga or Bluff. Because they are there; because to ordinary travellers they represent the boundaries between the known and *terra incognita*.

On past the gemstone beach and coal-mines of Granity the road turns inland and upwards — a long haul around the impossible buttress of Kongahu Point. We stopped there, high up above the silent bush and a sea that was silent, too, so far off did it glint. The road was ours. We saw no other traffic. We just idled in the warm sun before continuing over to Karamea, that oddment of climate and geography whose connection with civilisation is that one simple, arduous road over the Radiant Range. Visiting Karamea is like stepping into the sheltered warmth of a greenhouse, for, by some quirk, it has a subtropical climate.

Groves of nikau palms parallel the narrow road beyond, and in those groves, undulating gently along the sand dunes, the undergrowth was a brilliant canary yellow, for the lupins were blooming at their best.

We stood, hands in pockets, contemplative on the southern shore of the Kohaihai River. At our feet, round, moss-covered stones interspersed with spiky reeds bordered the deepening stream, its shoreline clarity colouring to amber, then umber. Across the stream, the hump of Kohaihai Bluff and that mystery land beyond, accessible only to trampers on the Heaphy Track.

Some time later we turned away to retrace our steps. Conscious of how much we'd missed. Aware that we could travel for infinity and still find new things.

But for the moment our odyssey was over.

Karangarua derelict.

216

Coronation Hall, Ross.

217

Aylmer Street home of Joseph Grimmond,
one-time mayor of Ross. Built in 1870.

Our Lady of the Alps, Franz Josef.

Okarito youth hostel.

Ross.

Okarito.

Near Franz Josef Glacier.

Jacksons on the Taramakau River.

Standard railway cottages at Otira.

Former Hokitika public library.

St Mary's, Hokitika.

222

McFarlane's Kumara Hotel.

223

Reefton.

Mrs Lawry's garden shed, 73 Shields Street — that was a good cup of tea!

Hunters' dog kennels at Reefton Station.

Shields Street, Reefton.

The 'European', Charleston; now gone. This photograph is our memorial to the passing of worthwhile historic buildings.

226

Denniston coal wagon.

**Denniston — at the top the
famous incline.**

Westport Municipal Chambers.

CHAMBERS

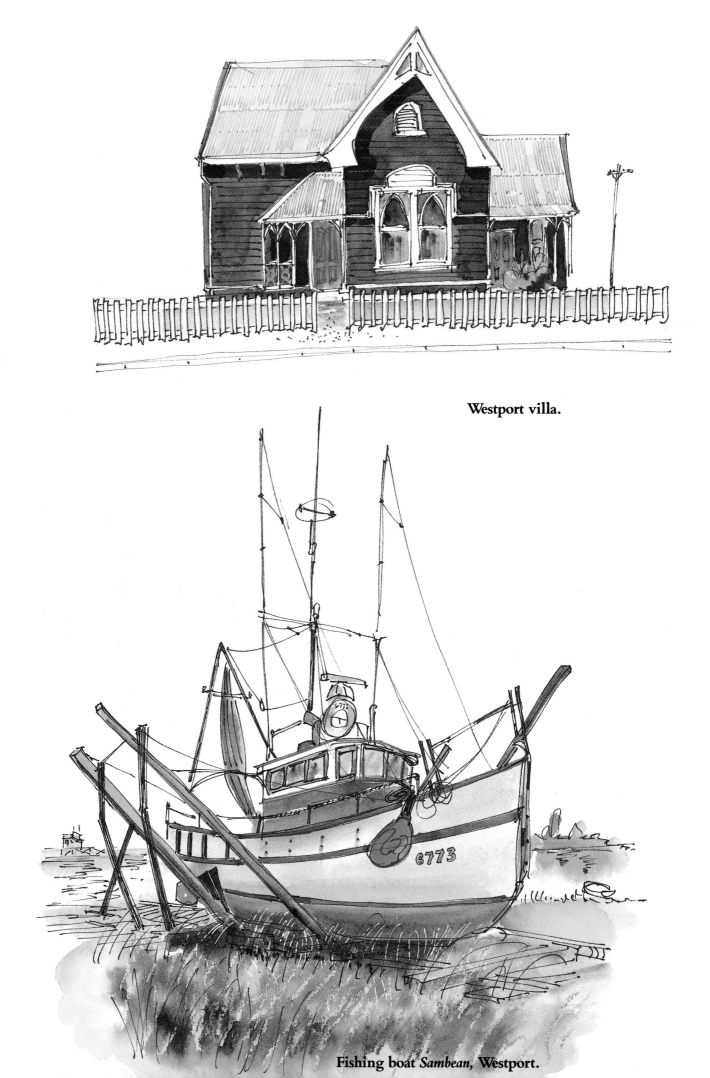

Westport villa.

Fishing boat *Sambean*, Westport.

'Granity' is not a description of the fast food. It was named after the large blocks of granite hereabouts.

Granity.

Kohaihai River mouth. The end of the road, and the start of the Heaphy Track.

231

The nikau grove just south of the Kohaihai River. In the end one of New Zealand's best benefits is the gift of remoteness. Here among these haughty palms there's just a slight breeze, the distant boom of surf, and peace to reflect on the privilege of living in New Zealand.

232

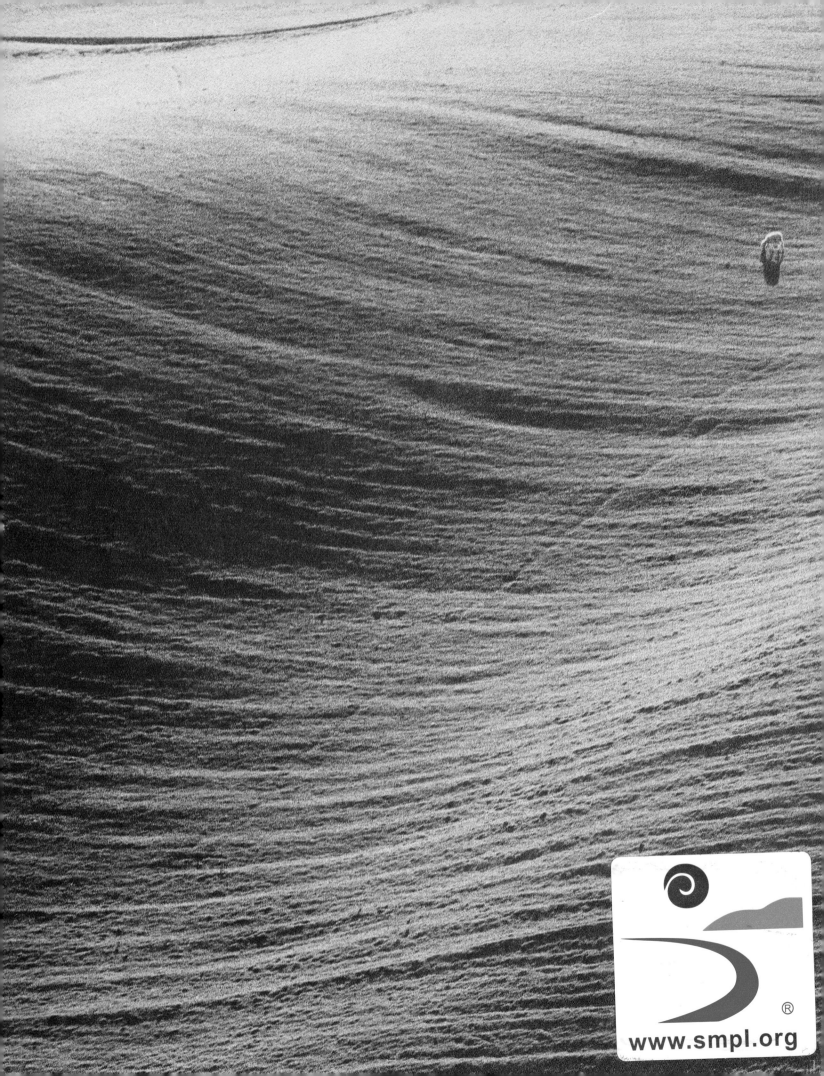